THEOREX

THEOREX
THE THEORY OF EXPERIENCE

PARIS
TOSEN

Canada

Theorex is a work of nonfiction.

ISBN: 978-1-926949-08-6

www.tosenbooks.ca

Book design and cover by Paris Tosen

CONTENTS

Introduction 1

Chapter One 9

Chapter Two 23

Chapter Three 27

Chapter Four 30

Chapter Five 35

Chapter Six 42

Chapter Seven 46

Chapter Eight 51

Chapter Nine 63

Chapter Ten 76

INTRODUCTION

What if there was only one pure day, half-bright and half-dark, that represented the totality of human existence, and what if this bipolar reality recycled itself repeatedly over the course of what is known as human history in a motion not unlike that of a grand pendulum. That would necessarily suggest that human history could have been no more than the multiple viewings of one succinct revolution, or halation, of a particular paradigm continuously replenished and redefined as and after each turn and all occurring within the context of one turn replayed. The wheel of life as it has often been called is much closer to the true nature of existence than ever before accepted. On one turn it rotates clockwise and on the second turn it rotates counterclockwise, all the while spinning on its axis to give the impression of a 360 degree revolution occurring over an extended time frame since each half-turn occurs in a different reference point. I introduce the concept of a halation instead of a revolution because the basic breath embedded in every living thing on Earth, must breathe, and composed of an inhalation and exhalation: a bright and a dark; an open and a close;

a yin and a yang; a heaven and a hell. The halation, or revolution, meditates change of form, but change of form does not include change of matter.

It is similar to taking kernels of wheat and churning them in a revolving mortar and pestle and turning it into wheat flour; then by adding water and salt and churning still we get dough. We cook the dough in a heated environment, or oven, and we receive bread, the staple of life. It is perhaps not by accident that bread has survived across all of human history as a irreducible food staple. The process of making bread is uncannily related to the process of making life. The idea being that life evolves, ie changes form and not matter, and enables humankind to progress. But, under these conditions, do we need to have time in order to realize our full potential or can the presence of a revolving day, a complete halation, imprint us with the same kind of result?

That is the level of question, grand question, I asked myself just before I began the formulation of a radical theory on the human experience. The idea that life is a journey is not new to most people. The idea that life might just be a static wheel revolving is also perhaps not new. When I looked for proof I decided that the most powerful evidence of truth is truth itself and truth is in the obvious, that is, in everyday life. If we look around we will note that the wheel is ubiquitous. Automobiles, motorcycles, bicycles, airplanes, strollers, skateboards and rollerblades all have wheels for movement. The buttons on your blouse are round. Wedding rings, intended for long term relationships, are circular. Eyes are circular. Companies use circular logos. Door handles are circular for the most part and even rotate. Elevator buttons are round. Gaming system controls are round. Circular theory is present in our daily experience enough to suggest that circular theory also predates our human experience. The Greek postulate that nothing comes from nothing is nothing new, so the proof that circles exist in our lives, to a large degree, also suggests that circles exist at other unseen levels. The influence of circular processes must have originated from another system of circular processes and may be evident in other higher dimensions yet inaccessible by everyday people.

As I continued to ask my grand question about the structure and composition of human experience I began to rethink the very structure and composition

of human experience. Some previous and
contemporary thinkers looked to human experiences
as something that shaped reality. I looked at
experience as something that fueled reality. Once
again I looked at the evidence of the obvious. The
world we see functions because of underlying sources
of energy. An automobile is propelled by the
combustion of oil-derived gasoline; a baby stroller by
a food-powered human; a mobile phone by a lithium
battery. And life, what propels life? By that I mean
what propels the attraction of a mate, the prospect of
a job, the desire to buy a certain kind of house, the
need to learn scuba diving, what propels us to move
from one location to the next or to study geometry
instead of business management. The grand question
then becomes what makes all the aspects of our life
function. And the amazing answer I have discovered
is experience.

This book will reveal in an unorthodox and
controversial manner the secret to human life, with a
focus on the scope and parameter of life with
experience as its fuel. Experience is the thing you go
through that influences your perception of the world
at large. Seeing a movie at a Cineplex is an
experience. Having unprotected sex is an experience.

Eating raw oysters is an experience. Playing video games is an experience. Going to work day after day is an experience. Killing someone is an experience as is the courtroom drama that might follow. But in the past, theorists viewed experience as simply a part of life that added to wisdom and decision making ability and directly related to maturity. Older people have accumulated more experience than younger people and this enables them to perceive life with an altogether different lens and an altogether different set of priorities.

What I'd like to suggest is that like an automobile the human vehicle also requires a fuel besides food. The fuel would be used to fuel that which exists beyond the body and has come to be known as consciousness. It is odd that after many thousands of years of extrapolation and discussion and despite the advanced technologies of the modern day, mankind is as close to understanding the complexities of consciousness as he is of curing stupidity. As most know, education cannot cure stupidity. The only thing that education can do is to increase knowledge. Stupidity is more correlated to ignorance than it is to knowledge and we know that the greater we can understand our level of ignorance the more knowledge we will have. Point is that mankind does not fully understand consciousness except to say that it is an intimate part of each of us, and all of us that provides the very backbone of our experiential life.

Ask a pure scientist and he will tell you that life is predictable. Ask a pure spiritualist and she will tell you that life is unpredictable. The scientist will tell you how you will die while the spiritualist will tell you how you can live. Perspective from different minds are rarely equal and this causes confusion in a stressful world loaded with mundane things such as taxes, illness and failing relationships. And yet perspective is a very important piece of the collective puzzle because perspective determines what you experience as the wheel of life revolves. As night and day fluctuate and we move within that cycle we require fuel in which to evolve, or expand. And since the consciousness is the very essence and primordial goo by which we are propelled then it is experience that is the ethereal fuel for our consciousnesses. The revolution of existence could be and will be here, viewed as a kind of existential, higher order game, but there are important pieces to this elaborate game and over the course of this work I will divulge in grim detail the mechanics of this experiential system that will ultimately question everything you ever believed about life, yet intuitively might have known.

Hypothesis: The body is a vehicle for generating a kind of spiritual energy and returning it to the source to complete its multiple cycles before being released or sent elsewhere in the system.

Manifestation is the total potential of a human life form in the modern composite reality exhibited through the divine being. All beings have the ability to manifest their ultimate reality. In fact all realities are manifested. It's the interaction between all manifestations that produces the result, the friction, the energy needed to propel lives forward. The manifestation of one singular reality would be ultimately static because there is nothing to interact with it. Humans choose other manifestations in order to develop and evolve their manifestations in order to progress. But there is danger is too much friction and bad interaction which can destroy the house of cards. Manifestations are both fragile and complex. Bad interactions, such as from negative manifestations and destructive ones can rob or suck the life energy of the individual and cause illness, stalls and career failures.

Ultimately all manifestations reach a climax, collapse and rebuild stronger (or weaker). All manifestations must be monitored once peak lives are reached in order to maintain stability. Failure to do so, in other words, failure to realize the final manifestation could result in life failure at a very high level.

CHAPTER ONE

Something comes from something. If we exist then
we have always existed; otherwise, we would have
come into existence and that would require us to
come from nothing, and *no thing* is not the same as
some thing. Likewise, if we were to stop existing then
we would go from *some thing* to *no thing* and then to
some new some thing, but something cannot come
from nothing. I see myself in a mirror; therefore, I
exist. I see my queen-sized bed; therefore, it exists. I
see a car, it exists. I see a window, it exists. I see, it
exists. See and it exists. If it exists then it has always
existed. The proof is ubiquitous. The proof is
omniscient. The proof is the sunshine streaming
down upon my face, permeating my flesh with
invisible nourishment, data for the unseen body. The
proof is the bumble bee buzzing by my right elbow as
it seeks out its precious pollen from a defenseless
dandelion. I smell the sweet summer grass and hear
the roar of four-stroke engines in the background.
Several canines run about the Vancouver city park
playing with colorful balls tossed by their respective
owners and retrieved by their respective pets. This is
life, a kind of life that seemingly looks fruitless on the

surface and yet is supposedly filled with meaning and purpose. The meaning of life is probably the most perplexing thing, next to programming a VCR or choosing a dress for the wedding. And yet somehow by some stroke of miracle VCRs work and weddings go on: people marry and people watch recorded programs. People move on and grow, have children and those children grow up through school, substance abuse and religious struggle. Life can be seen as a form of birth, growth, decline and death, or so at least that is what modern society accepts in their 80 year lifespan. I exist – but to what end? Am I just another product to be put through the cycle? Asking what is the meaning of life is like asking what is the purpose of a papaya or the meaning of masturbation. Without venturing on the side of vulgarity that would be interpreted as attention grabbing, I am essentially talking about the same thing as I will explain in detail over the course of this philosophical and theoretical work. There is purpose to life but I shall warn you that it may conflict with your present preconceptions of that truth. As much as we exist as separate entities we are actually the same entity under the same existential parameters. And since we exist then we will never cease to exist though may change in subtle ways. It is like the wind.

The wind blows across my face and where does it go?
Does the wind die? If we examine the wind we
understand it to be composed of air. And we live in
an environment filled with air (oxygen, nitrogen,
carbon monoxide). Air is a medium in which we can
interact. In this medium, as well as others, there are
certain rules and parameters specifically attached to
the medium. When wind dies it becomes part of the
air. The air doesn't die, if it did, we, as mortal
humans embedded with oxygen processors (ie
lungs), would likewise die. I exist and therefore I will
always exist. The question that might arise from this
analogy would go something like this: Are wind and
air the same thing or are they different?

The wind blows this way and that way, up and down,
fast and smooth and as it blows it seems to follow no
path or purpose except to freely express itself across
the natural and unnatural landscape. The wind is not
prejudiced against anything and nothing can hold the
wind. I look at the wind and I see freedom unlike any
other kind of freedom, an unbridled sense of the
spectacular. Air therefore – the supplier of wind – is
composed of a very powerful form of energy. This
form of energy is underutilized and overlooked and
has been this way for more years than humans can

remember. It is the closest thing to zero-point energy and yet it is the farthest thing from most minds. The energy I speak of is possibility: because from static air a wind may form and may become a desert tornado, or if it so happened, it would become a cool summer breeze. The wind may blow pollen off of fertile flowers to seed another landscape or it may rattle off the autumn leaves of a grand oak tree. The wind may flutter the dress of a beautiful woman to expose her undergarments or it may repel the cyclist rushing over the city bridge. The wind at its core is the purest expression of possibility. Why I speak of it is because just like the wind mortal humans also share this potent form of endless energy. Some have called them opportunities, chances, and choices. Whatever they are called the first step is to realize that they exist. They exist in everyday things and situations. For the purpose of illustration I shall call this analogy, choice.

I find myself at a grocery store shopping for some vegetables. Soon enough I find myself at the vegetable aisle and am confronted with an assortment of local and imported vegetables from onions to radicchio. I am presented, as another way to say it, with a choice of different possibilities. Will I buy zucchini or potatoes? Perhaps I'll take some iceberg lettuce, then again those organic tomatoes look very tantalizing. The only sense of logical footing I can rely on is related to my current needs, or tastes. At the fundamental level taste is a branch stemming from subconscious or intuitive needs that can either be helpful or harmful depending on your current health condition. Obviously this isn't a health book so my vegetable needs, or choice, follows some obvious set of circumstances. For example, had I had tomato salad last night I probably, not counting any strong craving for this particular salad, will not want to have a tomato salad for a second night in a row, but say if I had wanted a tomato salad last night and had no tomatoes then got stuck with a garden salad instead then tomatoes tonight would be a good choice. The past circumstance has impacted the present circumstance. I may be presented with a chance to regain a lost opportunity tomato salad. Now if in the future weekend I have invited some friends over for dinner and I knew that one of them actually loved my tomato salad then I may just buy the tomatoes now and save myself some time in the future.

For argument sake I buy the tomatoes so that I can make my salad. By buying the tomatoes I set in motion a series of other necessary choices because the salad also requires some oil, onions, salt and oregano. Once choice necessitates the presence of a host of other things, in this case food, in order to complete the possibility. Choice is only a piece of the construction, a brick in a wall that is used to form a whole possibility. What is a possibility? It is the completion of a series of choices that leads you onto other possibilities. By finishing the tomato salad, and eating it, I will have finalized and extracted the energy contained within the context of that possibility. That is to say I have absorbed that energy into my own being and expanded a part of my nutritional self. While I'd be the first to admit that human life is not a tomato salad, in no way meant to degrade the tomato, life does offer choices.

Choosing to start a new job necessitates a shift in lifestyle, perhaps casual wear becomes office wear, and slang turns into corporate speak. Whatever the case may be it remains a series of choices in order to gain the maximum value from the possibility. One cannot eat a new job in the physical sense, but one can experience and absorb the new job from the

interaction between new colleagues to finding ways
to spend the larger pay check. The spillover of that
choice, and I'm using a situation where a person
gains a better position with better income though
this may not always be the case, is that this person
has now expanded – expanded their circle of
influence, expanded their wardrobe, expanded their
learning situations, expanded their own sense of
confidence and improved esteem, expanded their
views of the world, expanded their craving for arts
and cultural things, expanded their interconnected-
ness in the global community. So by choosing to
upgrade their job they have ended up with an
expanded awareness, or, more essentially
consciousness.

 As I will show over the course of this work life is a
journey that fundamentally enables you to expand
your own sense of consciousness. The most prolific
example I can find to explain this and you will see it
throughout this book is the automotive metaphor.
Imagine yourself as the driver of a car, choose the
one you like it doesn't matter, and as you drive along
you notice something interesting out the side
window, you, of course, change course and head into
the direction of that interesting thing. You realize

you need fuel so you turn towards a fuel station, or where you think will be a fuel station. By doing so you will have made a choice by realizing the possibility; and what happens at the end of that possibility is hard to determine, ie you may not find the fuel station where you thought it should be or you may run out of fuel before you reach it.

Along the road you note that many stores and people and objects and situations and opportunities are being passed by. You always have that option to stop or turn as you prefer within the confines of the transit grid. Breaking the rules of the road can not have financial consequences but also can have personal ones as well. The obvious example is if during a u-turn you crumple a mommy and toddler. You have just caused a serious blip in your journey. Things may happen to your car despite your good behavior and intentions. Flat tires happen. A drunk driver may ram you. Or you might get a parking fine because you didn't have enough spare change.

The journey has an apparent goal, and may be as stupid as the answer to the question as to why the chicken crossed the road. Answer: to get to the other side. There is a profound truth in that statement as you will see and understand later on, but for now we are simply dealing with a moving car on a journey loaded with choices, the same as possibilities. At every stop, at every milestone, at every checkpoint you acquire things of value. Fuel has a certain value, groceries have a certain value, and dropping off a loved one at the concert has a certain value. And these values can be absorbed into your system. In the case of the car it is hard to notice the value of traveling daily to work except we could measure your hours worked and your rate of pay, ie your salary.

Your salary impacts other aspects of your life. One choice, to go to work daily, necessitates the presence and influence of other things. If we wanted to know something concrete about your journey, some proof, we would check the odometer smack dab in the middle the dashboard. The odometer is proof of movement along the journey. Now as you drive to work and make money you get married and have kids and buy things for your new house and go out for dinner or to the theatre or go to school or buy gifts and so on. As you move along your journey your world is expanding because you are expanding. Some lives expand less than others and as you will see this

does not need to be the case. But that is how
expansion works.

Before I continue with that I want to make a claim.
My claim is that expansion can work, not only in a
non-linear fashion, but also from a static position. I'll
explain here to illustrate the point. Have you ever
been in a car and suddenly you felt as if you were
moving even though your foot was firmly placed on
the brake pedal? The reason you thought you were
moving is because you noticed the large bus on your
side moving and therefore thought you were moving.
But in reality it was only the bus moving and not
your vehicle and it was the illusion that you were
moving that sent you scared. There was the
semblance of movement while you were stationary,
or static. The cinema and theatre has long used rear
screen projections with live actors cast in front to
give the illusion that an actor was in the situation
being projected on a screen. Project a large alien
spacecraft crash landing on the screen and have the
actors screaming in terror and diving for safety and
the effect is that it looks like the actors are actually in
front a crashing spaceship when in fact they are not.
The semblance of movement can inspire the feeling
of movement.

The car moves forward but the car doesn't need to move forward in a linear fashion. A car can, and I believe must, keep moving. A driver can view something to the side and turn in that direction, according to some basic rules, to experience that possibility. And they can keep moving in that direction or can turn again when so desired. The idea is that you must keep moving forward. Although you can backtrack if solely to re-fix your position. Going back is unhealthy over the long term and will not allow a person to expand as much as will force them to contract; that is the opposite of expansion, contraction, and, or, stagnation. This is highly undesirable. Stagnation is prevalent among the poor class and the undesirables. What is interesting to note is that poverty is not a fault of the rich class but a fault of the individual who is poverty stricken. What I mean by this is that if life is full, overflowing with choice and if a person, or group of people, keep choosing the same tomato from the grocer then it is of no fault of the grocer unless tomato is the only vegetable being offered. But as is the case in life there are more vegetables than is possible to actually measure since vegetable varieties are being manifest as and when needed, that is, as and when perception requires it.

This brings us back to the concept of possibility. If all possibilities exist loaded with experiential potential then why would people keep choosing from the same basket of goods? Why do some women repeatedly choose unfaithful men? Why do nicotine addicts keep smoking cigarettes? Why do failures keep failing and successors keep succeeding? I believe this is the case, and it is a complex one, of a misplaced perception. Have you ever played the road game of spot the car? This is where you and your friend, usually a sibling, play a game whereby each of you has to spot a certain make of car, maybe of a certain color as well. The one who spots the most first will win. It is a simple game that contains a very powerful truth about perception. By adjusting your perception you can spot whatever car make you have agreed on. After a point it becomes fun and ultimately it becomes boring. What is interesting is the fact that while you will have realized how many cars of that make are on the road you will have failed to see how many other makes of cars are on the road. As you gain experience and learn more about cars you can expand your choices. This is like in life where a child becomes a teenager and now has to think about sex whereas before all they were concerned with was Saturday morning cartoons. By high school you were thinking about which girl or guy to go out with. What allows you to do this is nothing new in science and I may be boring you with it here except that I think it is important to understand that perception are the goggles through which you find your choices. As you will see many things can affect your perception.

The only way to maximize the life journey is to move forward (illusory movement) and to explore all the possibilities related to your particular needs. Along the way you will finds things, people and objects, to help you on your journey. Collect them, cherish them, but do not attach to them because they are meant to help you. Along the way you will also meet others on the journey, other consciousnesses, and you can help each other. Remain detached and focused on the goal that remains as your personal experiences. When looking at life from afar we begin to get a glimpse of what it looks like. It begins to have a pattern. It begins to look like some network with a design, or logic, to it. We may not understand it at first but if we study it we understand why we did what we did and how it has impacted our journey. You may not understand the human nervous system but you must accept that it exists. You may not understand the silicon computer chip but you must accept that it powers your computer. You may not understand the pattern of your life, the non-linear pattern, but you must accept that you yourself exist. Something comes from something. And this something, this consciousness known as you, is traveling on an ontological non-linear road in order to gain experience so that it can expand, so that it can continue to expand. And this non-linear road could also be called a labyrinth.

CHAPTER TWO

Since its invention at the turn of the twentieth century the automobile has not only prevailed as man's reliable source of transportation, but, more importantly, the automobile has evolved and become the technologically advanced human propulsion device of the modern day. In its most simplistic acquaintance the automobile – be it the car, truck, jeep, van, mini-van, SUV – is comprised of the same essential parts necessary for its mobility. On the outside is a pleasing yet stylish appearance. A sports car is far removed from the jeep because the former is designed to interpret high speeds while the later negotiates with hills and valleys laden with mud and dirt whenever it can. A van may try to imitate a sports car and more often than not will fail because a van's intuitive nature is to haul goods and stuff of weight and volume (aka cargo); and, therefore, is not as efficient in attaining speed. To reach the greatest speed a vehicle needs the sleekest design, the most refined architecture and, of course, an engine to meet its needs. At the heart of all automobiles is the propulsion engine. No matter the fuel or fire upon

which it derives its force the engine nevertheless is
applying the same principles to the overall vehicle.

A smaller engine burns smaller amounts of fuel and
generates a lower level of propulsive force. Not all
cars are built for economical purposes and meaning,
such as transport trucks, needs heftier engines in
order to fulfill their needs. Besides the body and
engine an automobile owns a set of wheels separated
an equi-distance apart, two on each side. The wheels
can vary in size and interpret the torque generated by
the transmission. The wheels are basic idiot devices
without much intelligence of their own yet their need
to keep the automobile, vehicle, on the road plays a
vital role in the success of a vehicle. Remove the idiot
rubber tires and the most powerful and efficient
engine on the most appealing body is a standstill.
The wheels as legs are key to a mobile vehicle.
Besides the body, engine and wheels is the network
of architectured parts well integrated and fixed to fit
the vehicle of choice. Some parts and springs last
longer than others but all of them fade out sooner or
later. The rubber tires provide the asphalt traction to
the stop and go action of the other important, very
relevant, part of the automobile – the command

center. The dashboard is an invisible creation of
genius.

Not only does the dashboard and all its tiny little
controls provide feedback and basic information
about the vehicle but the dashboard also provides a
sense of life and comfort in the knowledge that the
automobile is a live and well. The dashboard is a sign
of life. The driver, by accessing and understanding
the data, can command the vehicle to suit his
immediate needs. In fact, oddly enough, even a non-
owner of the vehicle can command the vehicle by
accessing information off of the dashboard. It is the
greatest interface known to mankind in the obvious
sense and the most unassuming, even invisible,
visual tool. A speedometer, for example, not only
translates the current speed but also informs the
driver of the approximate time to reach his
destination; the safety level of his habits; the speed at
which fuel is used as higher speeds typically
consumer more; the relative dryness of the road; the
amount of distance required to come to a complete
stop; and the amount of his traffic time if he is pulled
over by the police. The odometer, a reader of mileage
and accumulated terrestrial distance, succinctly

explains the age of the vehicle, mostly the engine, and the therefore the value.

Mileage and age determine net value of the vehicle at time of consideration. Older vehicles tend to be valued lower, that is with high mileage, to the average user. Though it can be and should be said that certain collectors or admirers of older vehicles will pay a premium price for such automobiles. From the cigarette lighter to the stereo CD player to the gas and brake pedals, the dashboard is the best interface ever invented for the simplest human mind. One need not be of high intelligence to drive a car. One need not know the intricate operations of the valves and cylinders to drive fast. One need not even know where to put engine oil to drive. All one needs to learn is the dashboard and the basic voluntary controls such as steering and shifting the manual clutch. Automatic transmissions have even done away with the clutch so that an amateur need only turn the start key, shift into drive and steer at the desired speed, obtained by the gas pedal. If anything the automobile has become radically more complex behind the dashboard and radically simplified for the driver.

CHAPTER THREE

In order to accommodate the rising needs in society
to accept a declining religious stranglehold and to
prepare for a rise in spirituality the mind once again
needs to be stretched.

To be spiritual is only to be in connection to cosmic
and astral truths about reality and the make up of the
being known as human. Spirituality is but a word, a
mystical term that has only accomplished confusion,
fear and cognitive astigmatism. One cannot
experience all of life, that is to say energy as well,
without coming to terms with true existence. The
truest existence is manifestation – that all about us is
a manifestation, re-creation of what we need in order
to learn and grow; In order, in short, to experience
since ultimately that is pure truth. Pure truth is pure
experience. Nothing else is as relevant as that
statement. In fact nothing else exists except pure
experience that is boiled down from all experience.
That we as energetic and kinetic beings manifest all
good, bad and indifferent in our lives is a difficult
truth to accept and ones with lesser cosmic
understanding will refuse to accept such truth. At the

purest level of all things of source and creation is
pure truth. From pure truth all things spring forth
and become manifest in order to experience. But why
experience? Experience is a fancy term for
opportunity to grow and expand to a higher or more
robust or denser level than before. Experience
provides the necessary friction from which we all can
evolve as energetic beings. That is to say that we have
a simple mandate – on each cycle we must grow in
energy, free flowing energy so that at the end of the
cycle we return with greater, purer, better, more
refined energy than from when we started.

That is the result from pure experience and pure
truth. All that happens is not as relevant as all that
we become from it. The memory of experience is
irrelevant as is the past. The past is useless for it
brings no new learning unless the past experiences
weren't resolved and understood as past experience
that were designed for growth. Bad memories are a
painful way to say that there was no net energy gain
from the experience because what happened wasn't
understood and absorbed and this unfortunately
leaves stagnation and pollution is the energetic body
which then can pollute and weaken the human body;
despite the fact that the human organic body is quite

resilient it nonetheless breaks down with polluted energy that blocks vital pathways. Conversely, pure energy, if fully understood and accepted, could in fact make the body immortal. Because all bodies are manifestations: they simply exist as long as the consciousness wills it to exist or until the consciousness expands to a higher level and are ready to move on. The body is not limited by age, and, as you will see, age is a mental construction.

CHAPTER FOUR

Technologists are fervently putting together the
necessary pieces that will replicate the human being
except rather than of flesh and blood we will find
ourselves faced with artificial life. The latest proof, if
that can be used, is the video game console. The
video game console is essentially a machine designed
to play specially created games based on created
worlds where the physical player immerses himself
in a virtual player living in a limited virtual world. If
life is a mirror of other life, that is to say that the
human life we are living in this current moment
represents all the current moments across all lives so
much so that everything is equated by source and
result. As much as human beings believe that they
are special and unique the case remains that human
beings are redundant systems within an artificially
complex framework. There is constant proof to this
mess but the hypnotized minds led by false belief and
rigid civilian rules can no longer see the obvious
truth unless they have been awakened. The term
itself "awakened" simply means that the mind has
been dehypnotized. It is even perhaps possible that
minds are washed by technological invention

pervasive in the standard technology around such as TV, radio and print and now adding Internet to the mix. To suggest that men and women are being mind-fucked by some higher authority that is beneath government supervision seems a possible, probable explanation to the hypnotic phenomena so pervasive around the world. In addition, the media controls then perpetrates, facilitates and solidifies this hypnotic belief through media and word-of-mouth. It is in and of itself a great marketing coup. The people in turn feel that something is missing in their lives and it isn't the fact that something is missing as much as it is a fact that they are missing something.

$$1 = x + y + z$$
$$1 - z = x + y$$

wholeness = parts of human life represented as x, y, z

when z is taken away all that remains is x + y and z cannot be found.

In order for wholeness to return to one or 100% then we need to add z to wholeness which would cancel out the negative factor <u>and</u> we need to add z to x and

y. that is to say that in order to return people to an awakened state we need to add z twice.

The question one wonders is what that I factor represents, ie what is being missed? The z factor is obviousness. The obvious has been deleted from human minds in order to weaken the mind and to subvert the true intention of the human being. The only reason is for total subversion and manipulation of human beings for financial and political gain. It may seem like a small goal and ever poorly mislaid, but the human mind, when not connected to true spirit, is a very small, insignificant, fragile and childish thing. And that tiny mind will stop at nothing to protect is childishness. We must note that this is childishness nonetheless. It is important not to be superimposed by such lunacy for it is when lunatics make decisions that this reality is put in cosmic danger. Ultimately all things are *matterless*, that is they don't matter, that is *no thing matters*. There is no matter to speak of! But there is the opportunity to experience and grow and learn. That is the basis of life; The residual essence of pure experience.

This now returns us to the concept of mirrors of life, namely the video game console. It is not by chance that video games are becoming so popular and so extravagantly detailed. It is because mankind is reaching a level of science and technology that is allowing it to reflect itself purely. Mankind is now technologically able to build a perfect mirror with which to reflect truth and this will ultimately surpass the hypnotic state of people soon enough. But, but the mirror may cause man to split away from his true self instead of returning to his true self.

Video game consoles per se are machines that replicate human beings. It is far greater than a robot because while robots can perform work a video machine with a powerful game built-in can generate experience and since it is experience that is ultimately at the core of all things then the video game console can only be expected to become bigger and more complex until it reaches a sentient equivalent of human kind. It is at that point when man and machine will meet. It is at that experiential level that the mirror will be finished and man will face himself. What will happen when life itself is mirrored is unpredictable. In the past mankind has destroyed evidence of the mirror so that human kind could be protected and controlled. This time it is likely that the mirror will remain or at least affect more than one person and this will allow it to last even if shattered. The technological mirror is being built in many shapes and focus and it is only a matter of time that the human minds will become awakened.

CHAPTER FIVE

The Driver

Take any vehicle – scooter, airplane, train, automobile, bicycle – and there is one essential ingredient that is necessary, and that is the ingredient known as the driver or the pilot. In order for the vehicle to travel it requires a pilot to maneuver the vehicle because every road or path is uneven and is loaded with narrow twists and turns. And just like a race derby life is loaded with situations that call for quick decisions and rather than turning wheels of rubber or metallic wings the human vehicle works with things like emotion and anger. If anger is like the gas pedal then emotion is the steering wheel (say mood) and sorrow is the brake pedal and grief is the gear shift and happiness the horn. The human life has subconsciously reflected the spiritual symbolic meanings into the reality matrix. Matter is a reflection of antimatter and vice versa. That is why it is impossible to deny the presence of spirituality. The reflection of a spiritual life exists at all levels in the material world.

To deny that the spirit exists is to deny that the TV exists.

The driver of an automobile is a physical human being. For certain smaller automobiles a remote control unit could be used to control it, same with jet aircraft. This phenomena will likely increase as technologists master the art of unmanned vehicles. It is regardless in the scheme of life and only further supports my theory that a driver – be it a physical person or a remote unit – must control the vehicle. Remote driver vehicles have physical people controlling from afar. In the future artificial intelligence will replace the human but there remains a driver. One cannot escape the needs for a driver.

The human, as an organic-etheric machine, also has a driver. We have long called this Driver, consciousness. Consciousness may be associated as the spirit or soul or higher self or any other number of obligatory terms devised by men of power and science and all things artificial and essentially of non-truth. It is in the realm of mankind (including all genders) that life here was painted a certain color in order to subdue the will and cortex of the human brain. Humanity as a whole does not exist except as a formation of many bodies of uniquely shaped energy driven by an all-seeing, all-knowing, all-becoming source of truth known as consciousness. The consciousness itself exists outside of the reality plane and functions on the other non-local planes which essentially comprise the bulk of the universe. That is why life here is small and insignificant – it isn't compared to the starry skies, but, rather, compared to the other ontological space outside of this space. Consciousness is often confused with free will and awareness among other things and though science per se has yet to isolate the consciousness I can tell you that consciousness has little to do with free will and awareness. You may ask why and the answer I would summon would be like this: when you drive your automobile along a road there are a number of common items one finds. These include: traffic lights, sidewalks, lanes marked in the pavement, parked cars, pedestrian cyclists, speed limits and other vehicles among other things.

Surely you could, while driving, steer clear off the road into the sidewalk café or into the mother pushing her 6-month toddler in a buggy – or you could drive through the red stop light or heck, just stop in the middle of the road. You could do these things, but, but, you wouldn't. Why wouldn't you? Because you'd not only hurt and damage people and things but you hurt and damage yourself. Can you say that as a proud owner of an automobile that you have free will, ie that you can do what you want? That is also to say you can do it without consequence? That is what free will is. That is why free will has largely confused philosophers an brain scientists. Free will is a misnomer. Surely it exists, ie people do drive off the road and speed, and usually what happens is that people and buildings get damaged. In this sense we can say that free will doesn't exist as a benefit to human consciousness simply because it enables destructive options to be chosen. This is similar to meaning and purpose in that they only exist on paper. Life is meaningless and purposeless as you will understand over the course of this book. When we look at consciousness we find ourselves once again inside the car driving and at the same time noticing all things happening outside of the windows. We notice smiling faces and we notice the temperature of the weather, we feel the rain drops on our skin, we hear children crying and music being played – we are aware of these things and as much as we are aware we are unavoidably unfazed by such things. We are viewers and cannot interact and that is the one crucial difference between true consciousness, which doesn't yet exist in the vehicular world, is the point where vehicles, bodies, can interact. Consciousness, as much as it is the driver of mankind is also the point of interaction, that is to say the driver then becomes connected to other drivers and can exchange information and details and knowledge and can share. The automobile driver can step out of the vehicle and meet with other drivers to do this. But this has little to do with free will and awareness since those are obvious traits in an obvious reality. I will explain more about this when I explain the Law of Obviousness.

True consciousness is the power of connection because only in connection do we as etheric beings grow. The point of life is this little thing known as interaction. The human body and all things are made of matter that actually doesn't age except, except since it must in order for people to accept this reality. Imagine if there was no such thing as ageing. Imagine if time didn't exist. Imagine the value of life. How would life be measured? Consciousness itself is eternal and can only exist within the framework of eternal bodies. This does go against conventional wisdom that suggests that we are mortal but my argument here is that in essence I agree that we are mortal except our mortality exists only as part of our experiential learning. Physical ageing is a result of experiential learning and the readiness for the consciousness to move into the next cycle. It needed to do so but the mind of men and women has been trapped by the formation of unnatural laws such as pensions, age limits, voting rights, education, marriage and demographic power structures. In order to fit the unnatural restrictions placed on man the body has been made to suffer as a reminder that it is unnatural. It is unnatural to age. The body is matter, is energy and through energy may wane and whine, in structure and form it remains the same. Imagine the energy of an eternal battery that keeps regenerating itself. When connected to the extra ordinary world that most have yet to perceive there is a noticeable feeling of renewed energy fed by an eternal river of pure energy. Humans are hypnotized to believe in ageism in order to fit economic models forced onto society by the elite who wish to remain elite. When one person ages so too will another. When one person laughs so too will another. When one person cries so too will another. When one person ages so too will another. These are the same

things but of a different architecture. Age doesn't
exist in an eternal matrix, why would it? Why would
there be age if all things last indefinitely? How old is
the sky? Who cares. The sky has no age and we live
under the sky; therefore, are we not ageless?
Consciousness is like this. Consciousness, as the
driver or mankind, is ageless.

CHAPTER SIX

ABOUT VIBRATION

It seems that the old saying that birds of a feather
flock together is more true than ever when it comes
to human beings. Why is it that certain people, say
business people, tend to flock together more so than
say suits and scientists? Artists tend to understand
artists better than say history professors. Housewives
understand housewives. Mailmen understand
mailmen. Blue collar workers understand other blue
collar workers. Is it that similar kinds of people, that
is to say, similar kinds <u>or</u> similar minds tend to
understand each other or is there something else at
play?

When I first moved to mainland China I settled in
the city of Shanghai. At first I had a hard time to fit
in because of cultural and language differences but
more so I had trouble understanding their way of
thinking despite the fact that I had been involved in
the Chinese culture at the time. My daily practice of
Mandarin was easy compared to my daily practice of
understanding cultural ways and traditions. I often

offended people through my westernized more direct methods and though the Chinese understood that I was a foreigner it made it difficult to break through the friendship barrier that exists between all people. After several years I managed enough of the language and culture to understand the local people and because I was able to have my opinion represented and made headway with friendships. After I returned once more to Vancouver (my hometown) I found myself once again confronted with a deep misunderstanding of the local people – the same Canadians I grew up with most of my life. My thinking had shifted and we were thinking on a different wavelength. Not only that and outside of the cultural shock I found myself perfectly able to connect with Chinese people, far better than ever before I understood them. Later I began to see a connection between like minds.

It seems that we can shift wavelengths and this may be the only thing that makes us culturally and intellectually different. It is as if we were a radio and were on a different station, or wavelength. What is interesting to note then is if this is true then we can understand each other by adjusting our wavelength, by turning in and receiving the transmission. The same goes for business people or artists or cooks and perhaps this is the most unsettling part of this – if wavelength is connected to understanding, or learning, and we could tune into different wavelengths then I believe it is also true that we can learn a particular skill, say a language by tuning in, and, as well, business or scientific knowledge.

The human body is similar as any natural and living object. It is only different in that the human brain can demodulate specific information signals that enable unlimited abilities within the matrix.

The human body is emanating magnetic fields of energy of the biological kind. Magnetic fields permeate all natural things and can feed off of natural objects such as trees if frequency signal matches that of the object. Inanimate matter does not reenergize human body and can weaken body over time if not surrounded by natural objects to compensate for artificial influences.

The existence of energetic fields in the natural world does provide support for the probability that humans exist in a free energy, self-supporting environment to

which artificial fuels are both inferior and obviously
redundant.

CHAPTER SEVEN

MESSAGE IN A BODY

Each act of communication contains certain basic elements that are integral to success. The most obvious aspect of a communication is the presence of a message. A message contains, in its purest form, a concise content. Just like an email and a letter which contains certain words and attachments. Emails are sent from person to person via a special electronic address. Letters also travel except are transported by physical mailing systems including human carriers and are delivered to physical addresses, usually connected to an individual or family.

A message is essentially a packet of information. It is not be coincidence that systems for storing, retrieving and sending information, aka information technology, have become more prominent in the world today. If life reflects pure truth in the reality spectrum then humanities need to control information and to be able to increase the rapidity and richness of an exchange only points to something that we need to realize. We are replicating much of truth in order to see ourselves in the plasma mirror.

Any packet of information can contain many things such as were mentioned. Today's email can easily contain photo images, video images, artwork, ideas, music, sounds and other connections to the Internet or other individuals via personal emails. Until recently we've been limited to the size of the packet of information because of bandwidth problems and storage limitations, but that has all changed and cultures to change endlessly, so much that if we look into a distant future, not five years but fifty years taking into account even a fraction of today's rapid progress we begin to see that at some point bandwidth hits endless and storage reaches infinite space. What can happen then is all things and if perhaps that the human message, the biochemical packet of information, were to be able to be sent it would be sent with a lot of attachments including memory, personality, ego and mind all connected from an original sender known as pure consciousness.

Consciousness is equal to the meaning and purpose of one's life; the will to succeed, the force of action, as well as speed of accomplishments; plus learning as a function of life lessons and understanding. If we could say that the meaning and purpose of one's life really provides a direction and the will, force and speed achieves a certain distance of achievement and the learning is about the content then we could derive an equation like this:

Consciousness = direction + distance + content

All humans begin with a certain level of consciousness. This span of energy changes over course of lifespan. The impetus for this change, this expansion of energy, is from the sum of experiences. Consciousness then is the sum of all experiences.

The idea that consciousness is a form of energy and energy is the capacity of humans to achieve a purpose. If capacity is the same as the storage and transport of energy then consciousness has a new formula:

Consciousness = humans achieving purpose by storing and transmitting energy

If life is an illusion, as in humans as well; then purpose doesn't exist. By readjusting the formula we get:

Consciousness = storing and transmitting energy

If energy is equal to experience, that is to say that through our experience we grow as spiritual beings and see life in a new light then:

Consciousness = experience

Initial beginning of astral existence manifested in flesh is set in a particular paradigm. All humans are searching for particular clues, items, people, lessons, knowledge: in essence these are integral pieces of energy that propels them forward faster and with greater energy stored. Once the cycle is complete and rebirth is reached (ie death in one particular physical form) then a new cycle begins. The new cycle is simpler in scale but can be more advanced in level.

The human form is given greater psychic abilities and whatever is carried over from previous lives assuming that they gained all the necessary pieces. The more complete the learning the easier the

achievement. The intensity of energy increases until
the lifeform finally gains an extremely high level of
energy. The goal being to keep it without seepage or
leakage. That energy is then transferred to the source
being. All individual beings are encoded with
information.

All beings are messages. Messages are designed to
interact with each other. Messages combine to form
longer tales.

CHAPTER EIGHT

The formula to life

If consciousness is equal to experience then the
lifespan of the true consciousness (including
previous illusory lives) is equal to the sum of all
experiences. And experiences are really sources of
energy since that is what feeds consciousness. We
can also interchange the word consciousness with life
and god. They are interchangeable. And god and life
are at the very root of existence. Consciousness is the
very root of one's physical manifestation.

Consciousness = $\sqrt{\sum X}$, where X is equal to
experience

The value thereby derived is the frequency
(vibrational wavelength) of the human soul. The said
value will determine whether or not the entity
(energetic being) can expand to the next platform
(level) or must return once again to the same (or
lower) platform in order to try again. Ultimately all
energetic beings will expand, some will do so faster

and some slower. There is a natural attraction to the source and can happen easier during certain cycles.

This reality can be seen as a maze wherein an energetic being finds their multidimensional sources of energy which will do a certain amount of necessary work and then return to the source.

Godliness, god, life, energy, consciousness, soul, spirit, love, truth, spirituality, is equal to the root of all experience. This experience can be measured in a kind of non-linear odometer locked deep inside the psyche.

The level of consciousness determines the gear the etheric vehicle travels in. of course the higher the gear the faster or higher speeds the vehicle can attain. Not only that but higher gears allow access to ontological highways that the human eye cannot see but the subconscious eye can.

The purpose of life is essentially the pursuit of meaning and the pursuit of meaning determines the speed as well since this directly relates to the gas pedal.

Body = vehicle = message
God = consciousness = experience derivative
Experience = odometer
Consciousness = gear
Purpose = gas pedal
Fear = brake pedal

The fearful are slowed; the very fearful are stopped. Ones who can control fear can drive freely; that is can stop and slow hen necessary but aren't afraid to let go.

Attachments = dead weight of unnecessary objects in a vehicle

Free will = steering wheel
Emotion = engine
Personality = operating system

Etheric vehicle used to travel across time and space.

If time doesn't exist then what does? Moments. If time is in truth non-linear then what remains as time is the moment. We experience moment to moment that can be short as seconds or as long as years. The length of the moment depends on the experience. Each experience, no matter the complexity or level of it provides a piece of life or of consciousness thereby raising consciousness which is measured in vibrational wavelength.

If experience is dependent on momentary cycle and wavelength is a part of this then the wavelength is derived from the sum of all moments. But since the experience itself is comprised of many extraneous factors such as: junk data, unnecessary dialogue, distance of travel, etc then we need to account for this in the equation. It is just like driving to Disneyland. The long ride to the park precedes the 2-hour stay at the park and is followed by another long ride home. You'll not that the moment is quite long.

But if time itself is irrelevant then that moment is really a factor of the total travel. The experience includes a range of extraneous data. We need to wipe out the junk bits of information and can do so by squaring the net experience. Therefore a value of 25 would be the $\sqrt{25} = 5$. Five would be the net benefit, or addition, to life for a particular life body. What is taken into consideration here is the reality that as you increase the momentary experiences the life multiplication factor (LMF) actually slows down. For example, a net experience of 225 adds a value of 15. While 225 is 9-times greater than the previous 25 the result to life or consciousness is only 3-times greater. Similarly a net experience of 2,500 is only worth 50 LMF. In life it is common to gain an extraordinary amount of experience and yet by virtue of the formula the net benefit to the consciousness is decreasing. That is to say at first glance repeated experiences will not add significantly to an individual; that is also to say that it isn't necessary to experience so much in order to reach higher levels of consciousness according to this formula.

If that is indeed the case then there would have to be other factors preventing the growth of individuals which is outside of truth. What comes to mind is the mind itself. If the mind refused to accept certain experience or the learning derivative from that experience then that would account for the need to experience unnecessarily. The process of letting go then, of forgiveness itself, is what solves this spiritual dilemma. Why? Because according to the formula an individual doesn't need an enormous amount of LMF before it peters out and levels off. How much exactly is needed is hard to measure but would indeed be an interesting scientific experiment to test the life value of a group of people made up of different ages, careers and experience.

I think that in theory if it was measure it would amount to a small difference in individuals to suggest

essentially that the experiences in life aren't as
necessary as they seem and rather it is the mind that
is interfering with the divine signal to the source of
all humanitarian energy and this essentially is
restricting and polluting the systems and causing a
disturbing effect in the cycle of energetic
manifestation that is why life is increasingly
disturbing and it is why when people discover that
life itself isn't made to hand onto and rather was
made to let go of people will actually enjoy life more
than every before. Essentially, that is the purpose of
the life multiplication factor (LMF) or the purpose of
life or really the truth. For it is **truth that is equal
to the root of all experience**.

$$\mathbf{T} = \sqrt{\sum X}, \text{ where } \mathbf{T} \text{ is TRUTH}$$

What is truth? Some have said that truth is god and
god is what is left in the absence of evil. But as I have
said that god itself is a creation., an artificial face
constructed by humans in order to prolong meagerly
existence and to be subverted by elite powers;
therefore, god is false. What remains and exists in
everything is energy. That is ultimate truth. Truth is
energy. It is a difficult truth to accept that life and
humanity and earth is really a manifestation of

energy and that we are all here to expand our own
energetic structure, matrix. As energy we are carriers
of explicit and complex messages that serve other
parts of the whole structure, system. Each and every
single one is no less or no more important than
another as a true manifestation. This is a concept we
must all understand as I have tried to understand
because no matter what you do or what you are,
regardless of how you have done well or how badly
you have survived you are an integral and important
part of the whole and no less important or valuable
than another no matter your economic class or
intellectual level. In truth we all serve the whole
system and in truth, that is in energy, we are all
about harvesting and multiplying and raising levels
of energy. And where people have been misled is by
the elite class and artificial power structures and this
has led people astray. Although not in the context of
this work, artificial structures outside of god worship
could include money, beauty and literacy. These
kinds of artificial incumbents could and have
drastically shaped and disturbed energetic beings
and made men into criminal and made governments
into houses of power and control. That is why an
individual has been misled they can return to the

road of pure truth and return to what is known as innocence. By doing so they can finish and ascend.

Whatever the error or mistake it can be corrected by forgiveness and returning to the true path and this then means that no man or woman will ever be left behind. That is why I say that no matter the wrong, do the equivalent of right. Godliness after all serves the multiplication of your own energy, your own consciousness and enables you, from wherever you have fallen, to ascend to higher levels. Ascension is what happens when energy grows outside of its confines and returns to source only to be born again of source onto another cycle.

Life itself is neither difficult nor easy, fun nor sad, neither a struggle or a breeze; life itself is a journey of energetic transformation. Hold onto no one particular experience so that you may continue to experience all things so that you may grow since that is pure truth: the magnification of energy.

Ultimately that is the **Theory of Experience**. Experience is the key to energy. Experience is the essence of this life. In order to maximize your soul and consciousness you must submit to experience and not hold onto any one particular experience for fear of losing out on the next experience and delaying your own spiritual growth. Hanging on to a bad experience slows down your own speed of ascension. Your goal and each individual's goal is to ascend so that they may be magnified and then descend once again. The root of all experience allows that to happen and one not need to experience too much, ie ageism is a fallacy and retirement an artificial construction, in order to gain truth. And there is a final surprise and one which may be difficult to accept: Ascension and deccension can happen within the same vehicle. That is to say though reincarnation does play a role in life it need not to if people understand that this body of energy does not age and that age is part of time and therefore irrelevant. Age is irrelevant. If my theory is true and if proven over more stringent forms of experiment then this body can supposedly last indefinitely. This I must admit is difficult for me to accept because of years of programming, repetition and brainwashing that have proven otherwise. But if a person is also part of deeply rooted hypnotic suggestion then perhaps we as humans do not age. This would wreak havoc on our economic system of current but I believe that we can alter the economic model to accept immortal beings in a connected world. We are smart enough to do this and economies of the world are already moving in this direction, if only greed could be subverted.

Understand that all things in your life are distractions and that they are all wonderful. Understand that humanity, as earth, doesn't exist as does time. There is only energy and the desire of energy is to expand. Experience is the key to expansion.

Experience enables the body to expand consciousness. That is: increase the frequency of consciousness and decrease the wavelength. The purest consciousness is cosmic grade in frequency and wavelength.

ABOUT WAVELENGTH

Wavelength is central to many things: circle of friends or influence; skills and knowledge; and ability to shape, manifest, reality.

A particular skill, for example, is not based in repetitive skill understanding or practice, but rather it is based entirely on frequency tuning. Each skill or knowledge set exists and is being broadcast at a certain frequency and a person can access that knowledge set by tuning in more so than by work alone.

If this is true then even physical skills such as weight lifting or martial arts is attained through frequency modulation rather than purely by physical practice. This would contradict all modern and medical restrictions since it is assumed that a person requires the development of certain muscle groups and health status in order to practice martial arts. But if a mental skill like algebra could be gained by frequency modulation then it seems only natural that physical skills are also based on a similar proposition. That would ultimately defy the laws of physics but perhaps those laws of physics need revision and rethink.

If matter is essentially illusion then what size of muscle is required to lift another illusion? Answer: any amount that you believe. In the context of purity then true belief is no belief and if no belief exists, ie, that you need muscles of a certain size and strength, then perhaps it is still possible to achieve physical results without the old preconceived notions of musculature. Now if a person were to try this and immediately fail it would be because they have not removed belief from their system or perhaps they haven't reached the right vibration that can access the super set of physical laws, the ones that support my energetic field claims.

CHAPTER NINE

MIND AS MODEM

What intrigues me the most about the human body is the close connection between the mind and divinity. All of our connection to godliness, in all of its variant cultural personifications, is from the human mind or what are known as the human brain, part of the central nervous system. Science has yet to demystify the gray matter and all of its complex chemical interactions but they have fearlessly interfered with the production and assimilation of neurotransmitters and I believe have prematurely interjected on a complex biomagnetic device and could have done more harm over the long term by improperly addressing the source of imbalance and say mental illness rather than stepping back and further exploring the 3 pound device.

When a person prays to a god or a source of energy or what have you it is with the brain that the thoughts are sent out. Thought propels a prayer, a message, into the ether, the yet-to-be-fully-identified black space through which all manifestation and intention is processed, and that prayer reaches a particular destination, often called heaven, and may or may not receive a manifest response. The fact has always remained that a thought was sent out and sometimes were also received. There have been numerous cases, to which I will not go into depth here, about people hearing voices from spirit guides, angels and a god, as well as from deceased loved ones. Despite the presence of our incongruous quality of data an the failure of scientists to conclusively prove one truth over another one cannot deny that the brain does and can in fact receive messages. At the simplest level I can think of ideas, especially new ones, and sometimes called inspiration, but ideas are often believed to have been generated in the brain, perhaps like decisions as well (but this is another matter), when in fact from my own consciousness theory those ideas were received from an external or non-local source outside the obviousness of this linear false reality. Now if the brain can send out a message (eg prayer) and can receive information (eg idea) then it must also be able to process this information and data, that is to say to convert from one incoming signal, extrapolate the data and to translate or breakdown into a coherent language suitable to the individual's brain.

So what we have at the simplest level to work with here is an entirely new concept of how the human brain functions. The brain ca, outside of its regular functions, send or transmit, and receive yet unidentified forms of information and data an can process them into a coherent form suitable for modern life.

A similar kind of device, a technological one, in modern life is known as a modem. Many laptops and computers employ internal modems today, progressively wireless ones, to connect to the internet. Mobile phones have modems to connect to the telecom providers and therefore to connect to other mobile phones. Modems are prevalent around the world and their basic function is to transmit, receive and process information and data. It seems irrelevant to go into detail about the function of such a device and may be better for a future work but we remain with a truly unique perspective now on the brain. Rather then having to fixate on a be-all end-all storage and processing device we now have a biomolecular magnetic modem that can tap greater sources of energy non-locally.

Interestingly enough if you were to extract the brain with the stem and spine in tact you might find that what you hold there is a kind of ancient-looking symbol known as the rod or staff, or the symbol for the modern day antenna. The antenna to the divine source of all things. Perhaps the staff of god.

This is consistent with the brain at the top acting as the modem in a complex biological antenna that is connected to a non-local source of divine awareness.

If indeed this is true, and it may not be the first case of such surprise, then our current understandings of the brain as a storage and processing device falls flat and explains why mankind is limited in his approach to learning, knowledge and skill acquisition. We are simply using the interior frontal lobe, or forebrain, which is estimated to be a million times inferior the subconscious mind. The subconscious mind is intimately connected to the infinite field of knowledge. There are other parts to the brain that I may get into at another time.

What we are dealing with then is a biomagnetic device, modem, behind the skull plate that broadcasts magnetic fields from the mind to locations yet to be decided, but most certainly on some kind of ontological map in an infinite space far superior to the temporal cave we live in. Perhaps the cave man had a reference to his state of mind when the modem was first installed instead of his place of residence. If a modem was installed, or grown, in his skull then his brain would have grown in size and his acquisition of tools and knowledge would have increased.

The biomagnetic modem is attached to the biomechanical spine that is attached to the skin and bones of the body's 50 trillion conscious cells. What we are dealing with is the presence and proof of divine telephony. That we are, and need not be, anything more nor less than message carriers in a sea of messages in a community of reality called humanity. I may even suggest that the human vehicle is nothing more than a mobile telecommunications device whose soul purpose is to store, transmit and expand energy.

Modem essentially translates, or interprets, data. If human brain is a kind of biomechanical modem powered by electromagnetic energy then all that is interpreted and processed is data. That is to say that

what the human optical system views, absorbs as
electromagnetic data, really is structured
polymorphic refractory information; or in less
structured terms, what the eyes see is data
manifestation. It seems contradictory to believe that
we can alter our life and experiences by pure thought
since the real world that seems to exist outside of us
is very large and very intimate. Intimate to suggest
that it suits each individual and there are billions of
individuals. A reality systems that can satisfy an
exhorbitant amount of individual needs satisfying
them all at the same time with little cross over or loss
is not as likely to be possible as is if the optical
illusion known as reality is emanating from within
each individual and is projected on the matrix, likely
to exist as a black space, a multidimensional space
that can process the data demands of billions of
humans, plant and animals.

If the following equation is true:

> objective reality = matter interplay x filtration
> value/ willingness to participate

where matter interplay is the collective interaction of
all matter (and events) to satisfy all players and
filtration value is the strength of ego, reason and

dignity and belief to accept the reality presented. This is inversely related to the willingness of the viewer to participate since a participant who strongly rejects participation will have their reality compromised.

If the previous viewer equation is true then what we see is objective reality. That is we are presented with a reality that is seriously devoid of our specific personal preferences. For example, if we asked for a new car this request would be processed along with billions of other requests and it is unlikely that you would ever receive a new car. We know that the case is proven that some people who ask for money or help receive it. Often this is written under the term "miracle" since it doesn't happen often.

DEFINITION

Miracle – something that doesn't happen often or is hard to replicate in a structured, logical way of thought.

The fact remains that success breeds success and belief shapes your life in more ways than one. Though not in the parameter of this work to examine belief, or lack of belief, I think it has been shown conclusively in actual experience and actual evidence by the simple fact that the rich and successful are in fact rich and successful; that 4—storey office towers have proliferated worldwide; that some cancer patients experience complete remission; and that huge metallic birds can fly hundreds of passengers 30,000 feet in the air. This list of accomplishments is endless and seems pointless to list here. This to me is the result of belief. This then leads to my alternative formula to the Viewer Equation and that is the Projector Equation. The formula is as follows:

> Subjective reality = belief quotient (manifestation ability x luminescent processing power/willingness to participate)
>
> = B (ML/W)

where the belief quotient (B) is the actual belief value of the participant, that is and includes optical clarity, spiritual connection to divine source, and residual programming in neurochemical processes multiplied by the ability of the person to manifest the kind of reality they prefer which is derived from skill and experience. The product of manifestation ability and luminescent processing power, which is the processing power of the black space through which all manifestation occurs and this is a fixed rate since is part of the innate program. The value I have yet to derive. All of this is inversely related to once again the willingness of the individual to participate. Those unwilling or fearful will adversely affect their experience.

It is the subjective reality in the Projector Equation that seems most relevant to me. This would better support that we can affect the environment by consciousness rather than be victim to the environment.

But this then does lead into the two opposing forces of life: good and bad, light and dark, yin and yang, victim and hero, believer and skeptic, scientist and spiritualist. Ultimately, it is the co-joining of these opposing forces that make up the interplay in our created environment since it is obvious that both paradigms exist at the same time.

Ultimately, if we as a conscious species of beings want to improve or degrade the collective world environment then it seems only natural that we progressively subscribe to a Projector Equation, or what I call the **Law of Obviousness**:

Being = pureness quotient (proficiency x
refractive index/ willingness)

B = PQ (PR/W)

The **Pureness Quotient** (PQ) is measured in
vibrational purity. The purer the spiritual, truthful,
connection to the eternal then the actual value is x
and can range drastically.

Proficiency (P) is measured by skill and experience.

Refractive Index (R) is measured in refractory
points much like that used in a mirror. The figure is
fixed at 100.00 as percentile (1.00)

Willingness to **Participate** (W) is measured in
courage points. The greater the amount of fear and
unforgiven qualities the greater the likelihood that
the subjective reality will be sabotaged or
compromised in some way.

The result of those things provide a state of Being, B,
for a particular human/ consciousness. Where Being
does play an important role in this reality, and one
that is the most relevant roles is in the manifestation
of life experiences. Being attracts and presents

situations with unexpressed learning potential so
that by doing so an individual life, contained in an
eternal vehicle, can generate experience points; and
as they do climb levels, the attraction of fresh
learning potential with more advanced and
paradoxical potencies continues, and they become
more conscious.

So this is how consciousness is raised, when learning
potential is expressed repeatedly through Being. A
particular consciousness absorbs the potential
learning energy and expands their awareness in
current paradigm thereby becoming aware of things
not yet seen yet have existed all along. The raising
consciousness, integral to every human, actually
adjusts the clarity and focus of perception and it is
through perception in which they find new life clues
and learning potential, and, as well, how they
acknowledge that they have raised their
consciousness, if ever so slightly.

Sometimes a person expands too much and
collapses, but the situations collect around new
individuals and offer an opportunity to once again
raise consciousness. The Law of Obviousness is about
exposing truth to exist or at least to be measured

within the confines of a person's perception. The key
to implementing experience as a useful piece of
energy is by using it as consciousness fuel thereby
generating more energy within the structure.

Conductor – different levels of quality and
conductance based primarily on cognitive factors of
resistance, ie artificially manufactured impurities
expressed randomly and forcefully on the system.
Cognitive factors of resistance: ego, hate, worth, fear,
reason, logic, intelligence.

As long as the system is free of disease and damage,
usually associated with ego, hate, worth and fear
then the consciousness can expand and strive for
pure awareness. If there is disease then the system
will collapse temporarily, or, if serious, will self-
terminate; that is to say that the system will
systematically shut down prematurely.

Although all bodies maintain conductive ability it
seems to me that while criminals and degenerates, as
defined in modern colloquialisms and not prejudiced
here, seem to encompass or harbor larger qualities of
cognitive-level of resistance; namely worth, hate and
fear, they are also much closer to poverty, addiction

and meagerly subsidized living. This then also suggests if my theory is true that conductive capacity affects frequency and therefore ability to expand consciousness. It is similar to metal being a far better electrical conductor than wood, and rubber being lower still. If a degenerate being, a vagrant or homeless human, was equivalent to the material of rubber in conductive capacity then that person or section of society would essentially be unable to evolve their consciousness. Likewise if a body was equivalent to say pure silicon they would reach a superconductive capacity; and, therefore would be able to expand consciousness through the propagation of experience. It is not yet clear at this level what equates with what value of conductivity. But it does seem by all accounts that resistance exists at varying levels as if evidenced by the presence of poverty, knowledge and luxury. What is also similarly true is that a body, any body, can retool their level of vibrational energy by removing levels of resistance. For example, it is wonderful how a body can attain a better life as hate is let go. Hate as well as anger, dislike, jealousy and envy impede the pure frequency from repeating at the necessary level. Letting go of hate also removes resistance of the material being and therefore improves life function.

CHAPTER TEN

THE GAME OF LIFE

The video game business incorporates a very addictive and time-consuming approach to extracurricular entertainment. It is not by chance that video games have been so taken by the graphic wizardry of electronic games, especially so in recent years. Video games have become as or more pervasive than cinematic films around the world which I believe is a closer reflection to a situation of human life.

If we examine the three important aspects of a video game system (see diagram) we will note that a **hardware** and **software** combination is put together as part of the actual game and a player employs a **controller** to control the characters in the game. A viewing **window** of various sizes and levels of sharpness is added according to individual needs. The newest gaming devices use photorealistic graphic imaging and powerful processing mechanics to create close-to-real, or close to actual experience, environment for the ultimate experience. Again a controlling device, now wireless, has a number of relevant buttons to give as much control as necessary in order to succeed in the game.

The hardware is embedded with rich technology and operating software to drive the games engine, that is to play all of the quirks and schisms of the game. The hardware of today can process a tremendous amount of data and this seems to be increasing steadily. The game itself is an entirely created world where players choose or build characters that have certain roles and goals in that environment. Success is usually attained by survival and accomplishment whether it involves stealing money or killing people or eating magic mushrooms or earning experience point is irrelevant.

I do not see a need to go into any more detail about the game, but what seems interesting to me is how close a relationship between the game and life, between the game system and the human system. Since it is human engineers and technicians who have invented the gaming systems of today it is logically to conclude that at a subconscious level the game system is loosely based on the human system and has been hampered by technological innovation. In recent years, as technology has leaped forward, gaming systems have become power houses, loaded with more processing power than mainframe systems used to run entire corporations in the mid-twentieth century.

Humans have created the game systems for humans to play with, as they have created automobiles and mobile phones. These are inventions made by the minds and hands of man. It could be said that these are extensions of man in order for man to extend himself and to experience new pleasures.

If software runs the game system (hardware) then I believe that consciousness runs the human body; therefore, consciousness is software. Hardware is the body and its pre-loaded operational instructions which once again leads us to a mystery – where is the controller? Who is controlling the human game? Religious believers would say that god is at the helm, but as I have pointed out god is a human creation and as a singular omnipotent being doesn't exist. According to my own theoretical work the controller (player) is a divine, or eternal, form of you. In any game the character personifies the player that is takes on their quirks and habits, strengths and weaknesses, preferences and tastes. Therefore we can expect that the player of your human game is similar to you, except that they exist in another paradigm, inside of another biomolecular space, another plane of existence if a planar existence could be similar to the game player in the real world and the character in the game world. The connection is technological in our reality, but that is not to say that the other worldly connection is not technical in nature. Higher forms of technology can mimic magic and/or divine things. For example, a caveman who happens upon our modern time and is given a mobile phone might believe that it is a god device or some kind of elemental magic and yet to us as modern beings in this paradigm a mobile is a telephone with no wire and a battery.

So the player, the god, the divine being is somewhere in a field we have yet been able to reach as physical beings but at the astral level, as in projection and travel, perhaps they can be contacted and perhaps at certain wavelengths we can hear the voice of the controller. Perhaps this is what is said as god's voice. So we are part of a purposeless game except when it comes to one thing – experience.

Every game allows a character (and player) to reach higher levels and to acquire new weapons and tools according to amount of time and amount of acquired skill and experience. So therefore the totality of consciousness ability is once again found to be connected to experience. Experience determines the value of life and consciousness and go and truth and the most important part of the game because consciousness and our emotional vibration to it is the most powerful thing available to any form of being. That is to say that consciousness is the connection between the player and the character.

Consciousness is the bridge between the two and the more intimately connected players and characters are the more potent and effective they become inside of the matrix. Ultimately, if there is a goal to life it is that – to be close to the character and to be close to the player. That is ultimately the greatest joy is when the player is intimate with the character and this is largely determined by the root of all experience. It is what every player strives for – mastery of the game and character in order to dominate the game, in order to win, in order to succeed, in order to enjoy all there is to enjoy.

We are at our best when we are connected to our
player, to go if you will, to consciousness because
consciousness leads directly back to the other, divine
you. That is the connection. That is divinity.
Consciousness is the wireless connection.
Consciousness is part of you, the divine being who is
actually in control and has the most fun being in
control, not when the player isn't responding. That is
why all we have done in the world today has
separated us from god, from you, in order for the
characters to make decisions and to subvert the
world. I see other hands of energy involved in this
and may need more explanation in order to
understand what really has forced us out of control,
ie what kinds of energetic beings have done this, if
and where do they exist? They could be other players
involved who are trying to separate the connection
while the divine you is trying to rebuild the
connection.

Ultimately, I believe that this game of life is about
experiencing and learning since that is pure truth
and pure energy and that grants the clearest
consciousness and the clearest connection to your
own divine self and that is what we want: the purest
connection to godliness.

A technologically superior game machine is one in which the player can fully submerse themselves into the artificial environment, that is to suggest that the controller is no longer needed and that the system can accommodate high energy matter such as consciousness. It is about having a vehicle that can hold consciousness, light matter of a yet-to-be defined quality, and prevent unnecessary seepage. The control itself is buried, built-in, inside the vehicle, it is part of the vehicle. Consciousness then is much like gaming software; and is an extension of the player: consciousness and player are same. And if the human, you and me, are conscious then we are the same as the player.

What is unique about this cosmic game is that the environment, loaded with potential learning experiences, is created spontaneously. That is why we can affect time. In spontaneous creation and intention, time doesn't exist because there is no linear movement. Occurrences happen spontaneously. Somehow over progress, time was added to game and it has seemed to lock out key psychic functions. Perhaps the source of consciousness was blocked by cosmic occurrence or hacked into, regardless things were changed and we created our own power structures, but separate from the source we are incomplete and dangerous. That is why it is of utmost importance to reconnect to source.

www.ingramcontent.com/pod-product-compliance
Lightning Source LLC
Chambersburg PA
CBHW060344050426
42449CB00011B/2828